William Gifford Palgrave

Four Lectures on the Massacres of the Christians in Syria

William Gifford Palgrave

Four Lectures on the Massacres of the Christians in Syria

ISBN/EAN: 9783741178689

Manufactured in Europe, USA, Canada, Australia, Japa

Cover: Foto ©Thomas Meinert / pixelio.de

Manufactured and distributed by brebook publishing software
(www.brebook.com)

William Gifford Palgrave

Four Lectures on the Massacres of the Christians in Syria

FOUR LECTURES

ON THE

MASSACRES OF THE CHRISTIANS

IN SYRIA.

BY· THE

REV. FATHER PALGRAVE,

SYRIAN MISSIONARY.

LONDON:
RICHARDSON AND SON, 26, PATERNOSTER ROW;
9, CAPEL STREET, DUBLIN; AND DERBY.
MDCCCLXI.

Price 6d.

PREFACE.

As collections are still being made in many parts of England and Ireland for the suffering Christians of Syria, the following Pamphlet is offered to the Catholic public, to afford some additional information on the subject of the dreadful massacres which have lately devastated the Catholic Church in Syria. A Pamphlet on the subject, by Rev. FF. Palgrave and De Damas, will probably appear before long, but the present reprint purposes to be nothing more than a collection made of the four lectures given by Rev. F. Palgrave, in different parts of Ireland, taken from the notes of the reporters, who were present at these lectures, for the local press. It must be particularly remarked that the lectures were given on short notice, as opportunity offered, and without being previously written. Also, on account of the short stay of the Reverend Lecturer in this country, they have not been in any way corrected or revised by him.

LETTER OF HIS HOLINESS POPE PIUS IX.

TO THE MARONITE PATRIARCH OF ANTIOCH, AND HIS SUFFRAGAN
BISHOPS.

"To our venerable Brethren, Paul-Peter (Massad), Patriarch of
Antioch for the Maronites, and to seven other Bishops of his patriarchate:—Venerable Brothers, health and the apostolic benediction.

"By your letters, so full of sadness, that reached us on the 25th of
this month, we have learned, with much chagrin and anxiety, the
horrible atrocities committed on the faithful in your districts by the
detestable enemies of the Christian name, and the public newspapers
themselves have within the last few days given us the mournful
details. To so many other sorrows with which we were already
afflicted, the climax has been put by the harrowing spectacle of so
many convents and churches consumed by fire, so many villages
utterly destroyed by conflagration and the sword, so many sacred
objects unworthily robbed, this innumerable multitude of people of
every age, condition, and sex, in part horribly massacred, in part
compelled to flee, and seek a refuge somewhere against imminent
death, during which you yourselves, of which our heart has been
most sensible, have been exposed like many other Bishops, to the
constant danger of losing your lives, thanks to the unheard-of
cruelty of those infidels, whose rage was doubtless increased by the
idea of the partition of the Ottoman empire, enunciated so repeatedly
of late by the journals, and whose fury has bsen so suddenly directed
to the annihilation of the Christian nation. Alas! it is very
afflicting and deplorable that in our age more sympathy, and even
aid should be accorded to the workers of troubles and seditions,
than to the Christian peoples, who groan under the yoke of the
Turks and other barbarous nations—peoples for whose liberation
Europe, in former ages, undertook such formidable wars—to such
a degree that in the general assembly of a certain nation, certain
orators went so far as to praise and applaud a man, who, to the
contempt of all right and justice, is endeavouring everywhere to
overthrow religion and society. It is in this perverse manner people
come to think and act when they reject and condemn the Catholic
religion, the only one that leads to truth, the only one that teaches
it, the only one that can heal the wounds of society when diseased,
and sustain it and raise it up when it is fatigued and ready to succumb. How much is it to be wished that they, the most interested
in it, might recognise at last that if human society incurs some
peril, it is not from the Church of God, but from the enemies of the
Church themselves, who, if favoured, authorised, and assisted, are
accustomed to turn their arms against their own patrons in order
to ruin to its foundations all civil and religious power. Nevertheless, venerable brethren, we hope, with God's help, and before long,

in the inauguration of an era more favourable to the Christians of your parts, for the generous French nation and its government are preparing a large fleet to send to the succour of your country; in like manner other nations have already despatched armed vessels to defend their fellow-countrymen, and rescue them as it were from the fangs of wild beasts. We have not been ignorant of this glorious impulse; we have elicited it, as far as in us lay, by our exhortations, being ourselves urged by our paternal solicitude, and we have no doubt that it will increase, for the defence of your common safety and well-being. For the rest, be persuaded that, for our part, we share in your grief at the disasters that have befallen you, and whilst we hasten to send you a small sum in money, all that our own poverty permits us to bestow, in order to procure some alleviation of your misfortunes, we pray and entreat the Father of Mercies graciously to look down from the height of His throne of glory on this afflicted portion of the Lord's flock, and deign to restore and comfort it again in His goodness and clemency !

"May the immortal God, in whose hand are the hearts of kings, cause the most powerful Christian princes to be stirred up so as to check the efforts of infidels, lest the latter should take courage, and band themselves more and more for the destruction and ruin of the Christian name. May these same princes, lastly, be able to comprehend what a grave, what an extreme danger is threatening all society, unless they unite all their influence and force to subdue, here in Europe the audacity of the wicked, to baffle the attempts of these men who, as if animated with fresh fury, meditate and strive solely how to extinguish all religious sentiment in the soul, to confound all divine and human rights, and, by removing all notion of what is just and unjust, to make the society of men like a den of furious beasts. In the midst of the incredible overthrow of civil things, in the midst of such great dread of things to come, this sole thought consoles us, viz., that the faithful scattered throughout the land may raise to the throne of grace fervent and constant prayers, so as to render our God most clement, who in His turn will give us in His season the tranquillity we desire, in such guise that we may one day congratulate ourselves at the happy and brilliant result of our prayers, and return just thanks for so great a blessing to the Supreme Moderator of all things, the Guardian and Avenger of the Church. Rejoicing in this hope, my venerable brethren, we grant with our whole heart, to you and to your flock, our apostolic benediction, as the presage of a better future on earth, and as the pledge of blessed eternity.

" Given at Rome, near St. Peters, this 29th day of July, 1860, in the fifteenth year of our pontificate.

" Pius IX., Pope."

FOUR LECTURES

MASSACRES OF THE CHRISTIANS IN SYRIA.

LECTURE I.

(From Freeman's Journal.)

F. Palgrave expressed the pleasure he felt in having the opportunity of addressing an audience in the city of Dublin, composed of the members and friends of so admirable and useful an institution as the Catholic Young Men's Society. Although not personally acquainted with this society in Ireland or England, he had heard much of it, and he had himself attempted—not without success—to introduce it into Syria. A poor missionary for fifteen years amongst a people who did not understand English, and with whom he must communicate in their own tongue, it was not to be expected that his accent now was perfect, and he, therefore, claimed their indulgence on that account.

At the present moment, he continued, the eyes of all Europe, particularly of Catholic Europe, are turned with horror to the east. I have myself been a witness of horrors and desolations that chill the very blood to read of; I saw them with my own eyes, heard them with my own ears, and only escaped by the providence of God from being amongst the number of the victims. This narration is not necessary to evoke your sympathy for the Christians of Syria, for that sympathy already exists ; but I may be able to put you in possession of the true circumstances connected with the frightful events that have taken place in that country, concerning which you get intelligence only by piece-meal—by detached morsels, often incorrect, sometimes false, and altogether of a nature that gives no clear, or distinct view of the occurrences under consideration. Syria, by its geographical conditions, favours the development of different races. That long strip of country lining the east of the Mediterranean is divided first by a chain of mountains called the Lebanon range, running north and south. This district is principally inhabited by two nations, the Maronites and the Druses. Behind this is a spacious, splendid, and fertile plain, bounded by the Anti-Lebanon range of mountains, inhabited principally by Christians, mixed, however, with Mahomedans, schismatics, and a colony of Druses. Behind this range stretches the Syrian desert to the Euphrates; on the verge of the plain are the cities of Damascus and Aleppo. The Christian population of these districts are drowned, as it were, in a mass of the most fanatical Mahommedans that exist on the face of the earth. The Maronites are Catholics, united with the assemblage before me in the bonds of holy faith, having the same sacraments and laws, and differing only in the circumstance of their ritual, prayers, and ceremonies being in the ancient Syriac language, instead of Latin. They were the descendants of Syrian Catholics instructed by the Apostles.

In the 5th century a monstrous heresy was introduced amongst these Catholics. It was a denial of the Incarnation of our Blessed Lord, and an assertion that His life, His death, His resurrection, were merely phantasmagoria. A certain portion of the Syrian Catholics stood fast to the faith of their fathers, they were consequently made the subject of dreadful persecutions, which for two centuries were, perhaps, equalled only by the persecutions endured by the Catholics of Ireland. Numbers of the Syrian Catholics fled to the Lebanon, where they formed a body, and nation distinct from, and hostile to, the heretics. After some time, instead of reorganising their laws and customs, which had suffered from persecution, they chose, with the permission of the Holy See, a Patriarch whose name was Marone; hence they were called Maronites, and from that period to the present, a term of 1,200 years, the Maronites, with a constancy having few, if indeed any examples, have remained faithful to their faith and their God.

Now, as to the Druses. They are the most extraordinary people on the face of the earth; they are the Atheists of the East. From an intimate acquaintance with their sentiments, I can speak authoritatively of their belief. The Druses deny absolutely the existence of a Creator in Heaven, or of a Prophet or Redeemer on earth. They give their curse (God forgive me for saying it) equally to the religion of Moses and the religion of Mahommed, and hold that the happiness of man is in being free from all law and religion. It is wonderful that such monsters can exist, and more, that they should be not only an organised, but the most organised nation of the East, having an aristocracy to which they are subject, consisting of only five noble families.

Obedience to their chiefs alone has preserved the Druses, whose morality is expressed thus in their own language—" Everything done in secret is lawful—everything done in public is subject to religion and morality;" or, "if no one sees you, you may do as you choose." They are brave, but the Christians, after all, are more courageous, and better soldiers, considering their perils and persecutions.

The great plain is inhabited, too, by Greeks, one-third of them Greek Catholics, obedient to the Holy See. For 150 years—the date of the existence of these Greek Catholics—persecutions were upon them. In Aleppo once, twelve heads of families were beheaded for no other reason but that they were Catholics. The total population of Syria was about two and a half millions, of which one third were Christian. Having given you this outline of the country generally I will refer at once to the origin of the recent outbreak. The Christian powers saved the Turkish empire from threatened destruction by the taking of Sebastopol. Articles of treaties were then signed between the Sultan, and the Christian powers, by which the Christians in the East were raised from the abject condition of slaves, to the prerogatives of free men.—This change created hatred and jealousy amongst the Mahommedans, who could not restrain themselves when they found the Christian on the same footing as themselves, and saw the prosperity of the Christians—religion and civilisation spreading over the whole of Syria—new churches raised in every direction—schools opened in every town and village, and the Christians assuming great political importance. The bitter hatred of the Mahommedans quickly developed itself. In a few weeks a Mahommedan preacher, in the principal Mosque of a Syrian town, openly preached that it was permitted to destroy every Christian they could lay hands upon, saying it was insufferable that " these dogs should have so noble a place amongst dignified Mahommedans." This atrocious doctrine was publicly proclaimed throughout the whole of Syria: it was well known to the Turkish government, yet no measures were taken to repress it, no censure was given by that government. The Christians, with the knowledge of all this, felt, of course, that their safety rested on a sandy foundation, but they hoped that the Christian powers who gave them freedom would have maintained it to them in safety. Meanwhile, the work of darkness went on. In 1858, only 18 months after the treaty of Sebastopol, a meeting of Mahommedan authorities was held in the sacred city of the Turkish empire, the city of Ikimduni. I mention this fact upon the authority of an influential gentleman employed in the office of the English Consul at Beyrout, and I had it also from the Turks themselves. At this meeting were eleven heads or chiefs, one

coming from each of the great cities, such as Aleppo, Cairo, Beyrout, Damascus, Bagdad, &c. The deliberations of these eleven
chiefs lasted, I was informed, three days, and the object was to
see by what means the progress of Christianity could be stayed.
The conclusion come to was worthy to be written in letters of
blood. It was, that in order to ensure not only the prosperity,
but the very existence of the Mahommedan religion, it was necessary to exterminate every Christian, man, woman, and child, found
in the eastern Turkish empire—to drown the name of Christian in
blood. The chief solemnly confirmed this resolution, and each
returned to his own place, to propagate and carry out the murderous
design thus formed. A few months afterwards the first blow
was struck in the city of Jeddah, at the instigation of the chief of
Beyrout, with whom I was acquainted, and while the massacred victims were yet writhing in their agony there, the same
chief of Beyrout went to Mecca, the city of the pilgrims, and in
that centre of the Mahommedan religion made the pilgrims from
all parts of the East swear a solemn oath that, on their return to
their respective towns and villages, they would omit no means of
rising against, and massacring every Christian they could lay hands
upon. This fearful project is now being developed in 1860; it
was to have been carried out in 1858, but for various reasons was
delayed. These facts were not known in Europe, and it is well
that they should be stated now. It was impossible for the Turkish
government then to carry out their fiendish plans, as the Maronites
were too numerous in the neighbourhood of Mount Lebanon. The
Maronites were fine, active, vigorous men, such as I have seen in
Tipperary.

The first thing to be done was to weaken the Maronite nation.
This was worked out by sowing the seed of discord between the
nobles and the people. The Turkish Government succeeded in
depriving the Maronites of their chiefs, and instead of proper government, anarchy and disorder got in amongst them. This was all
brought about between the year 1858 and 1860, and in the beginning of the present year all was ready for the massacre of the
Christian population. Up to last Spring the Christians were aware
that their very existence was in peril. From the sense of their
danger they went to the Turkish governors, and asked them, in the
name of former and old friendship, for protection at least for their
wives and children. It was most dangerous for a priest, even at
that time, to go out in public. I myself had to fly, surrounded on every side by those who were anxious to take my
life, and meeting on my road the victims of the Druses, bleeding
from head to foot. The Turkish Government took their measures
for carrying out their fiendish projects. It might appear strange

that the Christians, so numerous, being at least one-fourth of the population, should be so easily overcome. The cause was this. The Turkish Government supplied the Druses with muskets, powder and shot, while if a musket was seen in the hands of a Christian it was taken from him, and if he was known to have powder and shot it was regarded as high treason. On one occasion I saw one hundred mules laden heavily with ammunition starting from the palace of the Turkish governor of Beyrout. I asked where the ammunition was going, and was informed that it was going to one of the Druse chiefs in the mountains: for these reasons, it was no wonder that the Christians in their defenceless position, should be defeated.

On the 27th of May, in this year, forty Christian villages in Syria were in a blaze, while the Druses, with savage and relentless barbarity, were cutting down the inhabitants, who were flying from their burning homes; in the midst of this scene of horror and carnage was the tent of the Turkish governor, surrounded by soldiers, and notwithstanding the solemn promises given to the consuls that the Christians should be protected, they were slaughtered by thousands.

To give an idea of the terror of the scenes which were enacted in Syria within a few months would surpass the power of human description. In an hospital of the convent belonging to the Sisters of Mercy at Beyrout (that blessed institution) I heard, from the breathing corpses who were there, the records of the perfidy and cold-blooded barbarity of the Turkish government. What did some of these people tell me of the Turkish governors? They received the Christians in their palaces, and swore on Mahomed, and on their own children that no harm should be done them. It was only required that they would not bear arms, and they in their Christian truth and simplicity relied on the truth of the promise which had been made to them, and laid down their arms. But what was the result? That while the Christians were in these very palaces they were given over to the assassins and murderers who surrounded these palaces, to be put to fearful and lingering deaths. One Christian whom I knew, to avoid the demons who sought his blood, jumped from the roof of the palace to the ground, where he lay senseless for three days amidst the heaps of corpses that surrounded the place. On recovering his senses he had to crawl on his hands and knees, for safety and shelter, to Beyrout. They who hear me can say what must be the feelings of a Christian on seeing the terrible sufferings a people endured for their holy religion, guilty of no fault, but making the sign of the cross. In a city in Syria, which had been in the possession of Christians who had given up their arms and ammunition, the slaughter of the Christian inhabitants has had, perhaps, no parallel, save in your own Drogheda or Wexford.

On the evening before the massacre, and before the hatchets of the Druses were stained by Christian blood, some of the ruffians, headed by Turkish soldiers, went to the house of the principal priest of the town—the vicar of the Bishop. They stripped him of his clothes, cut off his fingers one by one, and stuffed them into his mouth, saying " receive the body of Christ." It is unnecessary for me to say what cruel tortures these demons put the good and holy man to before they deprived him of life. The rev. lecturer gave a vivid description of the massacre in the city of Sida, where the Turkish soldiers went out to meet two thousand fugitive Christians and inhumanly butchered seventy-five of them in one hour, and left their bodies to be devoured by the dogs and vultures. When on one occasion the Turks saw the dogs tearing asunder the body of a Christian priest, they observed that " dogs should be eaten by dogs." The rev. lecturer gave a most appaling account of the massacre of the 11th of June, when he escaped to the mountains by all but a miracle. He referred to the burning down of forty Christian villages, which were one mass of flame, and spoke with startling eloquence of the miseries and privations to which the Christians had been subjected. He drew a vigorous and heart-rending picture of the desolation which was poured out on the country.

Amongst the long list of fiendish cruelties he gave one instance of a most respectable and accomplished man, who had been on terms of intimacy and friendship with a Turkish governor, and was in the habit of sitting at the same table with him. When the massacre commenced he went to the Turkish governor for protection. He was received with a demon-like smile. The Christian gentleman observed, " Is this the way you requite an old friendship?" The governor made no reply, but observed, " take away this dog." The Druses took him into the court-yard, when they held a consultation as to how they could inflict the greatest amount of torture upon him. At length one of them aimed a blow of a sabre at him, and, with an instinct for the preservation of his life, he raised up his hand, and the sword cut off his fingers. They next hacked the skin from his body, and cut the shape of a cross in his flesh, which they filled with powder, and set fire to it. They, with hellish cruelty, brought forth his wife, and held her in front of her agonised and bleeding husband. They next cut off his limbs one by one, cut out his tongue, and then sawed him in two, and put an end to his sufferings. His wife became a maniac, and imagined in her frenzy that she was wading up to her knees in blood. I will add but one word, continued F. Palgrave. When you hear of the measures taken by the Turks for the pacification of the country, and the punishment of the guilty, you must not believe it all, and what you do believe you should not regard as of the smallest importance as a safeguard for the lives of the Christians who remain in Syria. The beginning was come—the end is not far off. These demons are determined to carry on their work. I have it from their own lips that there will be no rest in Syria until the Christian name is exterminated, and only through God's mercy will this fatal design be frustrated. I beg the heartfelt prayers of the assemblage to Almighty God to save the Christian inhabitants of Syria and the Holy Land. Ireland has endured persecution for the faith for 300 years, and she can feel sympathy for Syria, which has endured persecution for 1,200 years in the midst of infidels, assassins, and murderers.

Having mentioned that the recent massacres were not only massacres inflicted upon the Christians in Syria, and stated that hundreds of them were murdered in Cairo and Damascus, the rev. lecturer announced that in a few days he would be on his return journey to Syria, to share the fortunes and the fate of the Christians who were still there. He had heard from the Archbishop of Dublin that it was intended shortly to make an appeal in Ireland for the Christians of Syria, to save them not only from temporal but eternal death, for kidnapping of the faithful was being practised there. He knew that this appeal would be answered by the Catholics of Ireland in the spirit they had always displayed where their faith was concerned. For himself, going back with joy to the country where he had laboured so many years, where he would remain with his colleagues while a Christian remained—he besought their prayers in his own behalf, and that of the Catholics of Syria.

LECTURE II.

DELIVERED TO THE ST. MUNCHIN'S YOUNG MEN'S SOCIETY, LIMERICK.

(From the Munster News.)

On rising to commence his address, F. Palgrave said that, before all things, he ought, in a manner, to apologise to that honourable assembly for having taken them at so short a notice, or, as he might say, unawares. It was not his intention to have given them the trouble, so to speak, of meeting together so unexpectedly. However, he hoped that their generosity and their kindly feeling would pardon that inconvenience, which was entirely unintended on his part. The reason was, the short time he had to remain in Ireland; but it was quite impossible for him to go through the city of Limerick without taking the occasion of addressing a few words to its respected population. For many reasons, of which he would now give them one,—he wished to address the citizens of Limerick, and that one was, on account of its being the first city in Ireland to manifest the sympathy of its inhabitants with the unhappy Christians of Syria, who had been so inhumanly murdered. On that account, he could not pass through their city without making its inhabitants acquainted with the real state of facts which had occurred in that country. Again, passing through a city which had given birth to such a body as the Young Mens' Society, it could not be permitted to him to leave them without affording them, as far as he could, that amount of instruction and information which Providence had enabled him to lay at their disposal.

It is a matter of very great importance, in all public affairs, he continued, that people should be always rightly informed of what is going on about them, because, from wrong information, wrong feelings and wrong judgments are formed; and those who desire to arrive at right conclusions should take care to be rightly informed on the questions upon which they are to come to a conclusion. The subject which we are met to consider this evening is a public one, and not only that, but one of intense interest to every Catholic mind. Because Syria happened to be in the east, and at the other side of the Mediterranean, do not suppose that this meeting has nothing in common with your own affairs. I will leave out of the question all political considerations. If reasons were wanting why this meeting should take an interest in it, one would be sufficient—and that was, that you are Christians—that you are Catholics, and, as such, you are one body in our holy religion. If one member of a body suffered, our Saviour Himself has told us that all the members must suffer. Therefore do not think of the Christians of Syria as if they were dwelling at the other end of the world, but regard them as if they were your own countrymen—born in the one country of our holy faith—nourished at the same breast of our holy mother the Church, and therefore, we should all take a common interest in one another. This might be said before any meeting, in any country, and in any place; but it should be especially said here in Limerick, because Limerick is a place to which Catholic Ireland would look up for an example, and would wish to know what was said there, and what was done there; and, again, it is most consistent with the aim of the honourable society which I have the pleasure of addressing, that this should take place amongst them, for the objects of the Young Mens' Society are the promotion of instruction and of religion—of gaining ground daily in information, enlightenment, and knowledge, and edifying and strengthening yourselves in the doctrines and practices of your holy faith.

In the first place, you may acquire knowledge—knowledge of lands, the people of which you are accustomed to regard as strangers; and what can be more calculated to strengthen you in your faith, and confirm you in the performance of your duty, than the example of those noble men who have laid down their lives for their faith, and to glorify God by their willing martyrdom? This I wished to relate in a country and a land, and among a people that can well sympathise with such. You (the Irish people) have yourselves gone through sufferings and persecutions on account of religion, and therefore you are the better able to appreciate the sufferings of others. Such was your lot in other times, and therefore you cannot but look upon what is happening in Syria as something like what happened in Ireland some hundred years ago. Every one is more or less acquainted in general with what has happened there, by letters, and the reports in the newspapers and otherwise. I had the honour of addressing a meeting in Dublin this week, and I imagine some of you may have become acquainted with what I stated on that occasion. However it will not be wrong in me to go over the subject again, not confining myself to the same details but entering on other matters in the broad and general subject. With the means of information you have in your hands, much has been so changed, and much has been so falsified—perhaps for some reasons, and perhaps for no reasons, or unintentionally, it will be my duty to state to you some facts with respect to the massacre in Syria. Many views of the question have been published, and these are put forward not by such a one, and such a one individually, but they have been countenanced and as it were confirmed in high places.

First it has been said the Christians themselves in Syria are a people of very indifferent character—a mean, degenerate, and cowardly race. That to my own knowledge has found its way into many papers; and, worse, perhaps, there have not been wanting men who have dared, in the face of the most evident truth, to assert that the origin of the war was on the side of the Christians, and that they were guilty of having been the original offenders. Again, others have attempted to favour different nations who had attacked them, such as Druses and Mahomedans, and by exaggerating their good qualities to diminish the sympathies of Europe with the sufferings of the Christians in Syria. These speeches and statements have not been kept in a corner, but have been published, so to say, on the very roofs of the city. Now, you yourselves as Irishmen, cannot adopt such views, and yet there may remain on your minds something like an idea that there was a want in the information before you, something which was not fully cleared up. The first of these calumnies, I have heard it with my own ears and seen it

uttered with my own eyes, was that the Catholics of Syria were
little worthy of European sympathy because of their degraded and
degenerate character. Well I might say the same language had been
held of the Catholics of other countries, perhaps of a country very
near us, but let that alone. I myself have lived among these
Catholics of Syria for many years, perhaps that which would be
called in ordinary phrase, the best part of a man's life, and therefore I am enabled to say, that on the whole surface of the globe,
on the whole earth from the east to the west, there could not be
found a race of human beings more worthy to bear the name of
Christians than the Catholics of Syria—men more capable of sus-
taining the glorious title of Christians, than the Catholics of Syria,
were nowhere to be found. We hear about Maronites, and we
hear about the Greeks, and we hear about the Syrians.

Who were the Maronites, for instance? They are a nation who
for twelve hundred years, under persecutions to which those of
Ireland itself were but a shadow, have maintained their faith and
their nationality, enduring and untainted to the present day. Are
such a people unworthy of your sympathy? For what reason are
they called Maronites? It is a national denomination of the
particular district of the country to which they belong, in the
same way as you would call a person a Connaught man, or a Limerick man; and a Connaught man, or a Limerick man may be as
good a Catholic, and thank God they are, as any other Catholic in
any country on the globe.

Again, take the Greek Catholics, and who are they?—a numerous body, nearly 60,000, who, having been engaged in the unhappy schism of the Greeks one hundred and fifty years since, have
of late opened their eyes to Catholic truth, and returned to obedience and union with the Holy See. They met with persecution
which attacked them in their employments, in their honour, and in
combating with which many of them had willingly laid down their
lives.

Again, take the Syrian Catholics, and who are they? They
also, not long since, from having been blinded in the darkness of
heresy and schism, have returned to the unity of holy faith, and
have maintained the pure doctrines of Catholicity to the present
day.

Now, to which does more honour belong, to those who have been
faithful under difficulties and persecutions, or to those who have
preserved their faith, and kept their religion without any obstacle
or impediment being put in their way. The massacres in Syria have
been carefully estimated, and may be very little more or less than
20,000 inhabitants of the country, not children nor women, but the
fathers of families, and who have left about 80,000 Catholic and

Christian inhabitants without houses or homes, without a field to till, without food to sustain life, without clothes, literally without anything. These unparalleled persecutions were brought about principally and entirely because of the spread of the Catholic religion and faith in Syria. Wherever God's Word went or spread, it is morally certain that there the devil will especially set himself to work to impede its progress, or overturn its effect in so far as his wicked agencies may be permitted to prevail. You have probably heard more or less about the manner in which the bloody conspiracy against the Catholics of Syria was brought about. Some two years since, the principal chiefs of Mahomedanism, that is of the Turkish government, met together to devise the entire extirpation of Christianity in Syria. In every mosque of that blinded faith of Mahomedanism, that object was announced openly, and it was there publicly proclaimed that it was lawful for any " true believer" to murder and slay a Christian, by any means he could do so. This was proclaimed in broad day-light, and in the presence of the officials of the Turkish government, who, by every means in their power, encouraged its being carried into effect.

One of the principal causes which excited such a deadly conspiracy was not merely the fact of increasing numbers or property of the Christians, though that assuredly was the case; neither was it the increased influence of Europeans, though that also was the case; but more than all these, it was beyond and above all, the increase of Catholicity and its spread in Syria and Greece, to an extent that is wonderful to contemplate. I myself, unworthy as I am of the employment and duties of a missionary Priest, had under my care at the moment of the outbreak sixteen schools for Catholic children, boys and girls, and these were extended up to the very limits of the desert. All of these schools had been founded within the last two years, others last year, and some of them only last winter. These facts were observed and known to everybody, and of course came within the cognizance of the Turkish Government authorities. In the same way I myself, in the course of the different missions I had to give through the country, had the unparalleled happiness of receiving into the bosom of the Catholic faith numbers of heretics and schismatics of these lands, and I often had to treat with whole villages on the subject of their return to Catholic unity, so much so that the matter was brought before the Mahomedan and Turkish governors of the country; and I know the Turkish governor to have given immense sums of money in the way of bribery to those who hindered the accession to Catholicity of those among the Mahomedan population who anxiously desired it, and in respect to whom I was engaged in missionary duties. If there was nothing else to create malignity in the mind

of an evil spirit or fiend, it would be sufficient to see those whom
he had expected to become his easy victims rescued from his grasp,
and entered into the safe and sanctifying bosom of Catholicity.
Mahomedanism is a system which is directly opposed to Christianity,
not alone to Christianity in one form or another in particular, but
to the whole of Christianity, or to whatever called itself Christian.
Consequently, in Syria the Turkish government was always favourable to schismatics and to heretics, rather than to Catholics, being
most opposed to what is most Christian.   There is another reason
for this.   The Catholics of whatever race, or to whatever country
they belonged, always turned their eyes to Rome as the seat and
centre of Catholic unity, as having there a common centre, a common mother, aye, and a most loving one too; who, while she consoles
and strengthens her children, cannot fail to render herself and them
equally obnoxious to those who would fain destroy and exterminate
her from off the face of the earth.   For that reason have we often
seen those who would desire to bind the Catholic mind under iron
despotism, first attack the Holy See, and the Holy Father.
Again, while Christianity in general was gaining ground, a certain treachery was silently working against every man in that
country who made the sign of the cross, and gaining strength
among their enemies.   I have heard a great many, even in Ireland
itself, and among those who sincerely wished for the success of the
right cause, say, at the same time, "After all, my dear friend, we
must allow that the Druses knew how to fight better than the
Christians; in all their attacks we have seen the Christians give in
at once." But I would reply, "My dear sir, if it was your lot to be
opposed by ten men, and supported by nobody, how would you be
likely to fare in the conflict which you might endeavour to carry
on single handed?"   Every effort was made by the Turkish Government to assist those who would butcher, destroy, and extirpate,
and every effort was used on the other hand, to weaken the Christians.   About a week before the outbreak took place, I myself saw
a hundred mules laden with powder, shot, and ammunition, leaving
the palace of the Turkish governor of the city of Beyrout, and
going towards Mount Lebanon.   I approached one of the Turkish
soldiers who was guarding them, and asked him where they were
taking all these, and the man was simple enough to answer me, that
they were taking it to such a place, the residence of one of the chiefs
of the Druses.   After this, and knowing that the Christians had no
security for their defence, I saw them coming into the city to buy
muskets and ammunition, and I saw the soldiers of the Turkish
Government take them from them when they sought to bring them
to their homes, under pretence that there was a general order to
let no arms go out from the city.   This was carried on for several

months before the outbreak, until the Christians were obliged to have recourse to the most strange inventions, and I wll tell one, although the circumstances may seem rather ludicrous. On one occasion when I was in the city a number of Christians united together to furnish themselves with muskets. They came to the city and bought their weapons, but the difficulty was how to get them to the mountains. And accordingly they hit on a remarkable device, which, if it happened in Ireland itself, I think could not be more ingenious. They went to a carpenter, and ordered from him a coffin for a very corpulent man, a man of large dimensions, and having procured it they placed in it the arms which they had purchased. They then covered it with a large black cloth or pall surmounted with a cross, and then one of the clergymen, who was in the secret, took up the position of one who, as it were, conducted the funeral arrangements, provided them with lighted candles and censers; then came numbers of pretended mourners, with handkerchiefs to their eyes, and in this manner they moved on, and he conducted them out of the city, and when they were clear of the surveillance of the Turkish soldiery, they opened the coffin, and the dead man arose to life. Now I have recounted this circumstance not to create amusement, but for instruction, and to show what difficulties the Christians had to prepare themselves for the attack, which they had every reason to expect was intended to be made against them. It was by base treachery the Christians were trodden down. The calamities which happened to the Catholic population of Syria were connived at by the Turkish Government, although the population considered themselves to be under the especial protection of the Porte. Several days before the outbreak the Catholic population had received an assurance from the Turkish Governor that nothing should happen to them, and that they might go about their occupations in perfect safety as usual.

On the eventful morning of the 7th of June, every labourer, every peasant of the town was at work in the fields; the shops were open, but few except old men, women, and children, remained in the town, and few of these men had arms. On a sudden, at a given signal, they were attacked by a body of about five thousand armed men. Not Druses only, for that name has so much prevailed that it has been forgotten that they did only about nine-tenths of the work of slaughter and devastation. When the attack commenced the Christians returned quickly to the town, seized their arms, sallied forth and drove off the assailants, whose numbers were five times as great as their own. They drove them at once out of the city, and maintained it safe for the whole of that day, but in the evening those ferocious villains sent forward messengers to gather help from every direction. They came together, and the next morning the town was surrounded by an assailing body of at least ten thousand armed men. Then the Christians, seeing themselves incapable of making an effective defence, deputed some of the principal inhabitants to wait on the Governor of the city, and claim the fulfilment of his promise, that they should receive protection. But, what had he been doing all this time? He and his soldiers remained within the palace and fortified barracks, and never moved hand or foot for the protection of the unhappy Christians. And what was his answer to the deputation? He swore upon his holy book, upon his life, upon God, and the prophet Mahomed, that they were in perfect safety, and that they had only to commit themselves to his care, and that he would not allow any one to attack them.—When they heard this answer, and saw that there would be no help for them unless they laid down their arms, they thought it better to surrender to him whom they deemed their natural protector, and who had, to their mind, confirmed his promises of protection with such solemn oaths. Then they laid down their arms, which were piled upon the barrack square. Well, before their eyes the Turkish soldiery took the arms that had been piled, and distributed them to the attacking soldiery at the gates of the town. Just before that, the Governor said to the Christians, "Enter into the barracks, and myself and my soldiers will protect you." They did come into the barracks, and in five minutes after the city was assailed, and what did the Governor do? He charged two cannons with powder only, and having fired them, that is, what was called blank cartridge, at the assailants, he discontinued even that, lest the smoke of it might impede their operations, and he sent word to the Christians that the cannon were unfit for any further use. The besiegers then rushed in through the gates, and the plunder of the city at once commenced. The Christians seeing the manner in which they were entrapped, then endeavoured to break open the gates of the barracks, and defend the persons of their wives and children, as best they might, or fall as became Christians and men in the almost hopeless endeavour; and some of them had almost made their way into the streets when they were fired upon by the Turkish soldiery at the gate, and laid in heaps of dead on the street, whilst those soldiers who had so inhumanly massacred them, called out to the remaining Christians within the barracks—" See the punishment of those who do not trust to the Turkish government." They then left them imprisoned within the fortress for four days, without food, without water—heaped, so to speak, one upon the other, in the interior of the Governor's palace, and it was not till after four days that the Druses and the Turks ventured to massacre those unarmed victims.

Now, can it be said, after such an example as this, that the Christians were unequal in courage and manliness to their assailants. In the town of Zathlee, which contained about fourteen thousand Christian inhabitants, all making the sign of the cross—for that is not confined to Catholics alone; other schismatic Christians still preserve many Catholic observances, such as publicly making the sign of the cross, the invocation of saints, having holy images; these are all common in the East to Catholics as well as to schismatics. At this time, having been myself employed in that city as a priest for two years, I established an institution resembling in a great degree your own honourable association. for young men, in which they should meet together from time to time, and have opportunities for the development of their intellect, the direction of their morals, and the strengthening of their faith. At the head of this society, in the town of Zathlee, was a young man of inestimable Christian character—one whose demeanour was singularly mild, affectionate, and unoffending, and whose character for peace and charity was such that I knew him to have surrendered a sum of money, which was claimed in the most wickedly wrongful manner as due of him, rather than go to law with the knave who made the unjust demand on him. There was scarcely a perfection of the Christian character but this young man was gifted with. A few days before the attack I said, rather jokingly, to this young man, "if the Druses attack the town we shall have your young men to defend it, and of course we shall see you at the head of them." He only smiled, and said, "When the time comes I shall know how to do my duty." Well, every day, for nine days, the circle of the assailants was narrowing around Zathlee. The whole of the great plains, known as the plains of Baalbec, were swarming with armed marauders and plunderers of every description. Two thousand horsemen, armed at every point, rode through the ripening harvest and destroyed it. First they could see the distant villages enveloped in lurid flames, and each day the burning and devastation approached them nearer and nearer. Then every other hour such of the wretched peasants as, by flight, from their burning homes, had escaped massacre sought refuge in the town, most of them naked, and many bleeding from head to foot from the cruel and barbarous wounds which they had received. They in the town still sheltered them, until they had, so to speak, in that besieged town, at least twenty thousand of these unhappy creatures, most of them, women and children. Every day the men of Zathlee, and at the head of them the Young Men's Association, fought with the greatest bravery, at one time opposing two hundred horsemen to two thousand of their besiegers, and even in that unequal contest coming off successfully. At last, the circle closed about them, and there remained nothing but the very walls of the place to defend. That was the day the city was taken when this young man he had spoken of as so quiet and so meek, was the first armed man to defend the entrance of the city, and remained there fighting until he literally remained alone, and before he left he had laid dead eight armed Druses, who had come to attack him, thinking that, as he remained alone, they had nothing to do but to slay him, and after this scene he actually shouldered his gun and walked back into the town. It was ever so; the men who were most faithful to their God were always the most faithful to their country.

But there was another kind of courage displayed by those persecuted Christians, which deserves not less to be recorded and applauded, that is, the courage of those who suffered martyrdom for their holy faith; those who, having no means of defending their lives, laid them down at the foot of the cross—the Priests butchered in the very act of administering the sacraments. I can give you an example, with the particulars of which I was myself well acquainted, for it happened in my own convent, and among all the bitter feelings which I ever experienced through life, the bitterest to me was, that I had not the honour and privilege of being one of those whose lives were sacrificed in that residence by the infuriated fanatics who attacked them. However, God saw fit that it should be otherwise. Two days before that slaughter occurred, acting upon orders from my superiors, I was obliged to quit the place; perhaps it was the will of God that I should go, in order that I might be spared to make known the sad tale in other parts of the Christian world. However, there remained in the convent the superior of it, a venerable old priest, of truly sanctified life and most edifying holiness of character: two other priests, and three lay brethren of the order, men in every sense of the word most worthy of esteem and respect from friend or foe. When they knew the assault was inevitable, they planted on the roof of the convent a banner—it was the French national flag, signifying that they claimed to be under the protection of that Power. When the Druses broke into the town, the first place they directed themselves to was this very convent, and it was ascertained afterwards that they had secret orders from the Turkish authorities to do so, and were assisted by them, for after the attack was over, the bodies of no less than seven Turkish soldiers were found at the gate of the convent. When they entered the building the first thing that struck their eyes was the flag, which they instantly tore down and trampled underfoot, and then they immediately broke into the church, where many hundreds of Catholics were assembled, principally old men, women, and children, and among them twenty-five men who had chosen a religious life, and whose whole labours were devoted to the service of religion, and the education of poor children, and four of whom were ordained priests belonging to the Society of Jesus; the rest were schoolmasters, and those who visited the sick, all of whom had taken refuge in the temple of the Lord, with no power to make resistance to their enemies, and no object but to prepare to meet death there, and, by offering up their lives on behalf of their Holy Faith, to qualify themselves to receive the martyr's crown.   Well, as I have said, no sooner had the sacrilegious assassins entered the convent, than the first part of it they broke into, with the fury of demons, was the church itself. Then, without deigning to fire a shot, or to draw a sabre on the congregated multitude, they rushed to the altar, tore down the cross, and destroyed the altar itself, and every symbol of religion that remained upon it. Behind the holy place were concealed twenty of the best of the children who frequented the schools. Could those Christian children, under the shelter of the altar, expect mercy from the infuriated mob? No, and they received none. They were inhumanly butchered, and their innocent blood flowed over the spot where they were accustomed to assist in the celebration of the most Holy Sacrifice. Then they turned on the lay brothers belonging to the convent, one of whom was a member of the highest Christian family in the town. He was standing nearly in the centre of the church, exhorting those about him to lay down their lives with confident assurance of the abounding mercy and love of their Divine Redeemer—to suffer martyrdom cheerfully in the service of Christ. Three of them presented their guns at him, and he opened his breast to receive their fire; when the bullets had entered it he fell on his knees, and, breathing a word of prayer, he yielded up his spirit.   Then one of the assassins who had fired at him, went to the rope of the church bell, and ringing it violently, called out to all present, in the language of the country, "Be you aware that it was I shot that Christian priest." There was besides a young man, a schoolmaster, in whom I took a special interest.   One of them came up to him, and raising a sabre over his uncovered head, he asked merely to be allowed to make the sign of the cross, but the words were scarcely uttered from his mouth when his head was cleft in pieces. They then rushed to the place where the superior and the priests had taken refuge, and just at the instant that he was pronouncing the words of absolution, and almost before the words of pardon had passed his lips, they placed him and his companions in a line, stripped them of their clothes, and hewed them to the ground, and left them stretched dead corpses on the roof. They then set fire to the convent beneath, and it was not until after all this hell work was done that they turned to distribute the plunder.

In the city of Damascus, I can tell you something of what occurred. In that city there was a very ancient convent of the Franciscan fathers, and amongst them was one who was designated as Parish Priest of the European Catholics in Damascus. I had the honour of being his personal friend, and indeed I esteem it a great honour to have been the friend of a holy martyr. That massacre was carried out by the slaying of eighty thousand Christians, and two thousand young Christian women and girls were carried off as the slaves of the Pashas and Mahomedan chiefs; that massacre caused the river that flowed through the city to run with Christian blood from end to end of its course, and the sky to blaze with lurid flames for miles around that ancient and venerable convent of the Fanciscan fathers which for centuries has been respected by every enemy. Yet that was the first place in the city that on this occasion was entered by the assailants of the Christians. There were seven priests and two lay brothers in it at the time, and among them was the venerable Father Angelo, of whom I have just spoken. The leaders of the armed soldiery at once directed themselves to the well-known rooms of Father Angelo, hoping by an enforced apostacy, under the terror of a frightful death, to gain a triumph for their creed, or else to quench their hate in his blood. When they found the aged Priest, they dragged him to the centre of the square, and there they had the audacious insolence to offer him, a Catholic European Priest, to spare his life if he would renounce his faith and deny his God, and they threatened him with the most frightful tortures in case he refused to do so. I know no other God, said he, than Christ, no other intercessor but His Virgin Mother, and no other sign but the sign of the Cross. Thereupon they put him to torture with all the refinements of cruelty which their hellish imagination could devise; they literally flayed off his skin and burned many portions of his body while life yet lingered in it; they even did more that could not be related, and when at length his soul had departed from its earthly tenement, they dragged what remained of his mutilated body through the streets of Damascus in triumph. In the same convent was a Maronite, belonging to a high family of the city; he fled to the house of God for refuge; the same infamous proposals were made to him that were made to Father Angelo, and he was threatened with instant assassination if he refused to accept them: what was his reply—" Fear not those who have only the power to destroy the body, but fear Him who after He has destroyed the body can cast the soul into hell fire," and he had scarcely uttered the words when he received the crown of martyrdom. They then flung his lifeless remains from the roof of the convent, so that they were impaled on the bayonets of the soldiery beneath. Could any one afford to deny to those of such a race who still survived these frightful calamities their warmest sympathy, and as far as they could afford it their generous assistance? I can tell them that unless help of a substantial kind is speedily given to the Christian population of Syria, help by means of the bayonet and the sword, they will be utterly swept off the face of the land. But I have my trust, and you have also, in the mercies of God, and in the merits of Christ, for their protection. And they further trusted in the intercession of those martyrs themselves who had just gone from among them, for at least ten thousand had died as martyrs—equally martyrs of the faith, as those who sealed their devotion to it in the early ages of the church. They trusted that God would not suffer His holy faith, which had burned so long and so luminously in that hallowed land, to be quenched in the blood of its children.

But while they admired, and looked up to, and sympathised with these noble men and women—for I might also have spoken of women who gave up their lives in the spirit of martyrs of their holy faith—I might tell you of two nuns of the order of St. Basil, one of whom was burned in the flames of her cell, and the other flung off the roof, and both cheerfully met death to prove themselves worthy of their holy vows. But, while you give these all your sympathy, and your praise, and your prayers, do not forget the state in which the country at present remains—do not forget the widows and the orphans who cover the face of Syria at this moment. In that part of the country where I was located, I was acquainted with almost every acre of it. It was the richest and most beautiful district of Syria—full of Christian villages and Catholic Churches and schools,—the very garden of Syria—its population flourishing in happiness and comfort—its fields waving with the ripening corn—the vineyards drooping with luxuriant vines—its plains of olives laden with the richest fruit. Of that whole district of country there does not remain at present standing one town or one village—not one hamlet, not one house in which the sign of the Cross is made. The whole have been burned or razed to the ground;—not a field of corn or an olive plantation but is trampled down or torn up; nothing is left of which a Christian could be called the master. From that land, at the moment I am speaking, at least eighty thousand of its inhabitants have been driven away by a persecution and desolation unparalleled even in Ireland itself in the days of Cromwell. They are now wandering among the barren rocks of Mount Lebanon, which alone Turkish tyranny has left as a refuge to the Christians, no doubt with the intention of soon consummating their bloody deeds in the total destruction of the hated race, but this, I fully believe, God will not permit. There they now are, those whom I and my fellow labourers have so often endeavoured to

feed ; they are wandering about without food, without clothing,
without shelter—without even a mat to cover their bodies by
night while lying on the ground. But would to God that was all.
The enemy of their holy faith desired the death of their souls even
more than the death of their bodies, having established among
them a system of purchasing souls of which, perhaps, you have heard
some examples in other places.   I do not fear for them to die,
but I fear lest they should be doomed to die as dishonoured apos-
tates.—Now, what I have endeavoured to explain is but a corner
of a very large picture—a picture drawn from rivers of human
blood, and lurid flames of burning human habitations.   I know the
response what I have stated will find in the minds of the people of
Limerick, and in the minds of all who have Irish hearts within
their bosoms, and that you will not deny to the Catholic people of
Syria whatever your sympathy or whatever your generosity can
afford.   For it is not them alone you assist by doing so—you assist
yourselves, and you assist the Saviour of mankind, who first hallowed and consecrated the Holy Land, from the day of His birth
until the end of all time.

LECTURE III.

The Rev. Mr. Palgrave said, that as the discourse he would have
to offer that evening was within the church, it need not be so
strictly of a secular character as that which he delivered in a public
building in their city the evening before last.   He might, therefore,
observe in the outset, that the persecutions and sufferings of the
Christians in Syria seemed to him in many respects analogous to
the sufferings of our Divine Lord in His last Passion.   While they
spoke of these wonderful things, which had convulsed the East, for
they were wonderful in their horrors, it was well they should consider what the effects of them would be likely to be.   For God's
providence would not have permitted such things to take place
without an end and a purpose therein.   He would not make any
other preface, for the few, but eloquent words, with which the
chairman opened the meeting, explained the object which had
assembled them that evening.
I will say, then, he continued, and I would not say it in any other
place but in a Catholic church, that the Passion of our Blessed Lord
and Redeemer, which was accomplished on Mount Calvary for our

redemption, was the image and example of what will happen in the Catholic Church to the end of ages; that, as our Lord suffered, that we should suffer also, and even the very circumstances which distinguished that Passion—every event we read of as having happened to our Blessed Redeemer on that day, will be repeated and defined to the end of time to the members of His Church—seeing that the members should be no better treated than the Head. When I repeat before a Catholic congregation in Ireland, thank God, it is not to your present experience, but to the experience of the past I appeal.

With respect to the events that happened in Syria, I was in the midst of them, from the beginning to the end, and these events have, in a most extraordinary manner, reproduced, and set before you, the very circumstances, as far as such a parallel may be drawn, which would strike you with horror and indignation, while you read them in connection with the Passion of our Blessed Lord. Not, God forbid, that I should attempt to draw a parallel between the sufferings of the Creator and the Creature. However, there was an example given then, and it has been followed out at the present day. You may recall three circumstances in the Passion of our Lord, which are to be found in the sufferings of the Christians in Syria. The first was, that immediately before the Jews and infidels seized on our Lord, there took place the greatest triumph and prosperity which our Lord, as man, met with in His triumphant entry into Jerusalem. Immediately before the horrible outbreak in Syria, which filled up the months of June and July last, the prosperity of the Catholics of the East was something without a parallel. Never had the Christians enjoyed such freedom or·such prosperity from the days of Mahomed. It was about the end of April, or the beginning of May, that I entered the town of Damascus, after a prosperous mission, and having had the consolation of seeing many Mahomedans and infidels received into the bosom of the Catholic Church. Under these circumstances, and full of joy at such results, I entered the town of Damascus. If you searched the whole of the earth, it would be impossible to find a more delightful city, and whatever could be said of it must fall short of describing adequately its beauty and its magnificence. It is situated in the midst of gardens and fruit trees, itself adorned with superb public-buildings; everything which art and luxury could effect is displayed in its costly grandeur, and it contained one hundred and fifty thousand inhabitants at the very least. In fact, there did not exist any city or town which could bear comparison with the beauty of Damascus. Now, in that town, the very richest and most beautiful part of it was the quarter occupied by the Christians, no less than twenty thousand of whom were within its walls at the time I speak of,

and there was not to be found in the whole of the city edifices to
vie with their Churches. The great Catholic Church in Damascus,
in which 1 have often preached, was one of the largest and finest
Catholic temples in all the East, and the convents and private
houses of the Christians were equally remarkable for their elegance.
A stranger, who entered Damascus in the beginning of June, would
at once have said it was a Christian rather than a Mahomedan town.

It was on the 30th of April that I was invited to preach the
first sermon at the opening of the Church, by the Bishop of the
Syrian Catholics, of course you understand by that those who employed the Syrian language. That Church was built in a part of
Damascus, where, from the time of Mahomed himself, no Christian
had been permitted to allow the sound of prayer to pass from his
lips, for the quarter was inhabited by the most untameable
Turcoman and Kurdish hordes, and never had a Christian church
existed in that quarter. It was only twenty days before the
flames consumed the villages of the Christians around, when I
myself preached the first sermon in that part of Damascus, and
the Catholic Bishop solemnised his first Mass at it. At the present,
if you searched for that church, you would not find even its
burned walls on the ground where it stood, such was the fury of
the fanatical wretches who attacked and demolished it; and if you
asked where was the Catholic bishop, who said that Mass—that was
now upwards of two months ago, and nothing has since been heard
of him, so that you may easily imagine what has been his fate.
If you asked where was the congregation—I know not, if one out
of ten of them is left alive at this moment, though I could give
an account of one family who were well known for their piety, for
their exactitude in religious duties and for everything that was
good and benevolent. This family numbered no less than three
sons and several daughters, and all of them, according to eastern
habits, instead of separating on their marriages, into different
families, as in Europe, all lived together, as their houses in that
country were sufficiently large to be divided into the habitations of
several families. The men of that family were the very heads of
the Catholics of Damascus. One of them escaped, more like a
dead than a living man, while those who remained were besieged in
their house night and day, suffering the horrors of famine, and
hearing the ferocious cries for their blood, of the butchers who
surrounded them, yet hoping, perhaps, that the massacre might be
stopped. On the third day the barbarous soldiery of the Turkish
government found their way into the house; the family were all
there, including the father and mother, and with them three of the
most influential Catholic clergymen of the city. When these
savages entered they began to perpetrate their villany by something

worse than death, and by torturing and butchering the priests who had taken refuge in the house; they then savagely murdered the sons of the old man, and dragged them one by one before his eyes, and it was not until he had seen his children, either butchered or dishonoured, worse than death, that they had the mercy to put an end to his own life.

Shortly before this outbreak, I was present in a large district containing at least six thousand peasantry, and all of them Christians. While I was there, the former Bishop having died, the people had chosen a new Bishop, and prepared to receive him with all pomp and splendour, and I, with other missionaries, had the honour of receiving him. The whole mass of the Christian population in their gayest dresses, bearing crosses high in the air, and carrying banners on which they had inscribed the names of Jesus and Mary, went forth to meet their new Bishop. Had you asked me shortly after this where that Bishop was—He was in the Greek church of Damascus, when the barbarians broke into it. That church contained four Bishops, and amongst them this very Bishop whom I have mentioned, besides a number of clergy. Of these, only one prelate escaped, who was obliged to strip off his episcopal vestments and make his way out of the city in the disguise of a beggar, stripped half naked, and in that state he was obliged to wander about for two days and two nights, amid burning houses, and not having where to lay his head. It is certain that the day the Lord and Redeemer was triumphantly received in Jerusalem was followed by the agony of Calvary, and something of the same kind occurred in the case which I have just stated. I could tell you that of my own knowledge, being at the moment of the outbreak in the large town of Zathlee, the largest entirely Christian town in the whole of Syria. After having witnessed the plunder and massacre in that town, and the burning of all the villages through the country, I was only able to make my way from it disguised in the dress of a Bedouin Arab, and after having got a short distance from the town, I had to pass the fire of those very Turks and Druses, and nothing saved me under God's providence, but that they believed that I was not a Christian priest but a Bedouin Arab, and some of them were heard to say after they returned, that they fired upon a person whom they mistook for a Christian priest, but who was one of their friends. However, no less than five of my companions of the order of St. Ignatius, who were with me in Zathlee, obtained the crown of martyrdom a few days after that event.

One of the principal features in the Passion of our Blessed Lord, was the abominable treachery, and refusing of all justice in the manner in which He was condemned to death. Do you discover that there was nearly a parallel of the Passion of our Blessed Lord in the history of these atrocities in Syria?

It was but four days after the most solemn assurance of tranquillity and safety had been given them, that the country, south of Mount Lebanon, was bathed in blood or scathed with fire, so that in the whole district there remained not a convent, nor a church, nor a Christian house standing. At that time there prevailed in the city of Beyrout, where I had taken refuge, a most wild excitement, and a most fanatic movement of the Mahomedans in the town, aided by numerous Druses not yet satiated with Christian blood, and among whom there existed such a maddening fury for the lives of the Christians, that they were not sure of their existence for half an hour together. They could not know when they rose in the morning, whether they would be alive to lie down in the evening. It was during that time we saw arrive in the port one morning two large vessels of war; we had some hopes that they were European ships, but we found they were Turkish ships, bringing troops under the pretence of restoring peace and tranquillity to the country. No sooner had these troops disembarked, than our convent was thronged with women and children, and all who were unable to defend themselves. At first it was proclaimed, in order to excite the fanatical passions of the people, that a Christian had murdered a Turk in the midst of the city. And, in fact, the corpse of a Mahomedan was exhibited in the streets. Immediately, every one of the Mahomedans armed themselves. There was no evidence whatever to show how this man met his death, or whether any Christian whatever had anything to do with it. But the voices of the infidels declared that the Christians had murdered him, and the cry was raised that they would have the blood of the Christians, and would not leave one of the hated race in the city. While these events were going on, a young man in the position of a writer, or clerk, in a public office, happened to be passing by the place where the body of the Turk lay, and they seized on him and declared that he was the murderer. They led him into a house which was near the scene of the murder, and there assembled all the Mahomedans, the consuls, and all those who were keeping the peace of the town. The dead man was brought in and laid in the midst, and the prisoner, with his hands tied behind his back, confronted with two children, one of them eight years old, and the other nine, and their statement was taken, upon which was to depend the life or death of that man. Upon being questioned they declared they did not know who was the man that killed the other, but that his hair was a light colour, and that he was blind of one eye. Now, the Christian who was arrested did not correspond with this description at all, save having a slight defect in one eye. Yet they took him out of the meeting and ordered him to be shot, and as the children were coming' out, the Turkish sentry took out of each of their hands a piece of gold, which they had received as the price of their false testimony. During the trial, when the Consul of France remonstrated on the imperfectness of the evidence, and against the condemnation that was about to be pronounced, some of the Turkish authorities rushed upon him, and threatened him with instant death if he attempted to stand in the way of their predetermined purpose. There remained yet one act to be done that they might complete their iniquity. The governor of Beyrout has no right to order a sentence of death to be carried out without the authority of the governor of the province. But the governors secretly drew up a paper in which it was stated, that in cases of great emergency it was permissible to carry the sentence of death into effect. The Christian then said, " All I can say is, that I am happy to die for the quiet and security of my fellow-Christians of the town, and I hope my blood will content you." After this they bound him still more securely, and conveyed him to the public gaol; some spat upon him, and the soldiers ill-treated him in every way that could occur to them. He begged that he might have the consolation of a priest to prepare him for death, but that was denied him, it being the object of the Mahomedans to destroy the soul as well as the body; but in this they did not succeed, for the man who willingly offers himself as martyr for the faith, receives absolution from God Himself.

I was seated on the roof of the convent looking at the spot where the execution was to take place: it was eight o'clock in the evening when the large prison doors were thrown open. The authorities descended by the light of torches into the public place of execution. Two lines of soldiery were then formed, who insulted and struck the Christian, as he passed between them along the market-place. Arrived there, they made him kneel down, and the chief magistrate read a paper which declared that this Christian having been found guilty of a most horrible murder, must satisfy justice by his death. Once more the Christian begged that a priest might be allowed, to pray with him, and some Christians rushed into the convent, begging that some one of them would go to him. The first of the fathers whom they met went with them, but when he arrived the soldiery repelled him, and would not allow him to get to the prisoner. After this, the first of the soldiers approached, and, drawing his sabre, he struck the man with it as though he would have cut off his head at a blow, and gashed him deeply on the shoulder; the next soldier followed in the same way, so did the third, fourth, and fifth, and so on, and then when he fell exhausted, and hacked to

death, no description could give an idea of the savage yells which
succeeded. Next day the Mahomedans proclaimed that they well
knew the Christian to be innocent, and that they now demanded
the blood of ten Christians more. However, they left the body
hewed in pieces in the market-place, and on the second day after,
the Christians obtained it by stealth, and gave it Christian
burial. Now, many are the circumstances which assimilated the
death of this man with that of our Blessed Lord. He fell a willing victim against all law and justice, to a most excruciating torture
and death, in order to save his fellow-Christians. I will give
you another instance. There was in Mount Lebanon a large and
lovely convent, known as the Convent of our Lord. This was inhabited by Catholic monks, and supplied priests to those who had
occasion for their services. About three or four days after the
occurrence I have related, they received a letter from the chief of
the Druses, stating that there was great danger of an outbreak,
but, as far as he was able to defend them, there was no fear of
anything happening to them, but as some danger might arise, he
would advise them, if they had anything precious, such as gold or
silver vessels, relics, and the like, to put them together and hide
them in a safe place. They read the letter and sent back the mes-
senger with presents and thanks, and they thought to themselves,
this man has been always our friend and protector, and we may
confide in him—the advice he gives seems to be judicious. They
resolved to send and procure two labourers to help them to dig
under the pavement of the church, in a place which no one should
know but themselves. At a little distance from the convent
they saw four men standing. They wished them good morning, and
asked if they were employed by anybody; finding they were not, they
engaged them to open the hiding-place near the great altar, which
they did to a depth of about six or seven feet, and then reset the
pavement in its place. They were not aware that these four men
had been sent by the chief of the Druses to watch their move-
ments, and give him all the information he required. Next day,
while they were assembled in the refectory, a cry was raised that a
select band of the Druses was about to attack them. They rose
to escape, and had not the Druses gone direct to the church to open
the treasure-place, not one of them would have escaped with life.

However, the greater number did not succeed in effecting their
escape, eight of them stained the pavement of the church with
their life's blood. You are already acquainted with the general
outlines of these horrible massacres, and I will spare you the pain
of listening to further details.

Herod and Pilate, the Jews and the Gentiles, the Sadducees and
the Pharisees, all united together against our Blessed Lord to tor-

ture Him, and nail Him to the cross, and the same happened to the Christians in the massacre of Syria ; it thrills me with horror to think of the analogy as I witnessed those later barbarities. There were no villages in all Syria so prosperous as the Christian villages, no church so beautiful as theirs.

Now, after the outbreak they present such a spectacle as a ship affords when stranded on a rocky coast, disappearing in the yeast of the waves. Thus, when they left the town of Zahlee, the plain around it was thronged with Druses and Mahomedans, Kurds, Bedouins, and every other kind of pillagers. These Mahomedans were believers in the unity of God, but denied the Trinity, and the Divinity of our Blessed Lord. The Druses are real professed atheists, who deny the existence of a Creator, or of a prophet, and declare openly that there is no God in heaven, and no divine law upon earth. Now, these and the Mahomedans were always at war, and yet he saw them side by side, united together in the massacre of the Christians. They were always at deadly war with each other; they would not even eat together, or sit together, and yet on this occasion they were seen side by side, when they entered for the sack and plunder, and destruction of the town of Zahlee, and the massacre of its Christian population. Other tribes, whom we had not even heard of at all, united against us, and numbers of the bodies of Christians, weltering in their gore, were found two days after, under the blackened and blood-stained walls of our convent, by the Christians who went to seek for them, in order to give them Christian burial. They found the bodies of no less than seven of our (the Jesuit) order, murdered under these walls, and it was only by wearing the disguise of Druses that they were enabled to carry them away, the extermination of all the Christians indiscriminately having been determined upon. An universal rising against the Catholic religion in China, in India, in the East of Europe, seemed to have broken out simultaneously. But let us recognize it, and treasure it up as proof of the veracity and holiness of our blessed religion, for a stronger proof of it could not be given than that frightful persecution which the Christians in Syria so heroically endured.

You in Ireland rejoice that to a certain degree you are more flourishing, more free in the exercise of your holy faith than you were some years ago. On every side new churches and new schools are rising among you, and the Divine mysteries of our holy religion are allowed to be celebrated, unimpeded by any hindrance or interruption. Let us, then, thank God for it, and remember that God grants prosperity in order that we may be prepared for adversity. He grants days of rest in order that we may be prepared for days of labour. Let us then be always ready, and remember

3

that such a day may come when we least expect it. If we try
to serve our God and Saviour, and to keep our fellow-Christians
firm in their faith, and holy in life, as I am happy to say the
greater number of our fellow-Christians in Syria are, whom it has
been the will of God to have visited with this great temporal cala-
mity, but which He knows best how to turn to advantage for their
eternal account, according to the submissive and martyr-like manner in which they have borne the afflicting visitation, and recognized
the Divine Hand from which it came. Let us remember that
the Almighty Lord and Master of all would cling on the last day
to those who have clung to Him on earth. Those to whom the
temptation was offered of abandoning their faith, were exposed to
the alternative of instant death, because if a Christian was once
enrolled among the followers of Mahomet, he could not return
to the Christian faith except by submitting to suffer martyrdom
immediately. Whatever Catholic faith and Catholic sympathy
can do in sustainment of these poor Christians, will be readily
sent through safe and proper channels, for their benefit, through
the venerated Bishop of their diocese, and will be conveyed to
them through sure channels, and tend to saving them, not
only from temporal death, but from eternal death to their souls.
He who saves a soul from death receives from God the remission of
his own sins, however numerous they may be. And now God's
blessing be with you all, and remember me in your prayers.

LECTURE IV.

DELIVERED IN CORK.

*(From the short-hand notes taken by the Reporter of the
Cork Examiner.)*

After having the singular honour and great happiness of addressing an Irish popular audience, not only in the capital of
this country, but also in other places, and being on the eve,
although very reluctantly I assure you, of leaving the emerald
isle, I could not pass over the opportunity which your kindness,
your sympathy, your generosity and good feeling accord me, and
more especially the kind good feeling of that eminent association—
the Young Men's Society of Cork, to whom in an especial manner
we owe our meeting together this evening. I could not pass
all this over without doing my best, at any rate as far as in
me lies, to meet the wishes of your kind and generous hearts by

addressing you in a few words, for the limits of our time will not allow us more, which may suffice, as far as I can, to lay before you, and set in a clear light, certain matters connected with the late, or, perhaps I had better have said the present events in Syria, which have arrested so much of our attention, whether we view them as Europeans, as Christians, as Catholics, or, indeed, as men. It is impossible for us at the present time to be ignorant of all that we hear, and all that we read, of what is going on in the land of Syria and Palestine. And that for many reasons, inasmuch as it is the most ancient land on earth, the very land on which man was created, the first land mentioned in holy writ, the land of Abraham, of Job, and of other great and holy men, the land which has been sanctified by our Blessed Lord, by his Virgin Mother, and by his holy apostles; the land that gave birth to those to whom we ourselves owe all that we have of doctrine, of learning, I might almost say of the faith, since all the apostles, all the teachers of our holy church have come from it. How can we be indifferent to the misfortunes, the calamities, that have befallen that land?

We know, indeed, that for many years, indeed for centuries, these lands have, so to speak, been under especial tribulations; under persecutions and troubles, and perils, greater than have been endured in any other part of the world, whether for their severity, or their duration. At the same time, in the whole of its past history, from the time when the sword of Mahomet was first raised over the heads of the Christians of Syria, when they first bowed their heads to receive his yoke, never had they to go through such severe tribulations as they have undergone, or are at present suffering. And can we ourselves, Catholics and Christians as we are, our hearts and feelings stirred by the events that are going on around us, can we shut our feelings and sympathies to the misery and suffering of our eastern brethren? Though we have now in a time of peace and prosperity everything, by God's mercy, though deeds of cruelty and oppression are not now felt as they were felt in this very land, yet you are well aware of the great dangers and troubles which beset our holy religion, our faith, our church, even the very head of that church in the person of the Holy Father himself, while we are assembled here this evening. And for that reason, ladies and gentlemen, I think it is well that we should consider whatever can increase at the same time our knowledge and our sympathy, by the communication of that knowledge, and information respecting the Christians and Catholics of other lands, and awaken for them in our own breasts, those kind and generous feelings, which, whilst they may be productive of assistance to them, will, at the same time, react on ourselves with a healthful influence. And for that reason, ladies and gentlemen, without further preface, for the time we have would not allow me to speak at great length, nor is it necessary that I should, I will proceed to my subject.

It is not my intention, on the present occasion, to give an entire sketch of all the events which have occurred in Syria for the space of the last three months, such a sketch would be impossible. Not even the whole of this night, not even the length of three nights, not even the space of three months during which these events occurred, would suffice to relate to you all that has happened in the Holy Land. Nor do I intend to enter into many of the harrowing details with which I suppose you are all more or less acquainted, whether from piecemeal and partial accounts, viewed through the diminishing glass, not the exaggerating one, of part of the British press. Besides, you may all have become acquainted with those events painted in true colours, though far short of the reality, which have within the last few days obtained publicity partly through my unworthy means. However, I should imagine, that none of you will be unwilling to hear an account of those events from one who, I may say, witnessed them; for, after all, what we hear gives more satisfaction than what we read, and the spoken word is infinitely more effective than the written word. The written word is a dead language; the spoken word has in it the power of life. For that reason I shall lay before you a few of the principal circumstances that led to this outbreak in the East, and whatever else may seem to me capable of instructing, interesting, and edifying you; and this all the more because I have the honour of addressing, in an especial manner, the members of the Young Men's Association, an association that has for its object the enlightening and edifying man, the enlightening of his mind and the strengthening of his heart.

I suppose you are all well acquainted with the Ottoman empire, and how the Turkish government first conquered Syria by the sword about 340 years since, at the beginning of the sixteenth century. At that time Syria was equally divided between a Christian and a Mahometan population. When the Turkish or Ottoman empire took possession of Syria, they found it governed by Mahometans, but these were not foreign oppressors, and there is a great difference between domestic and foreign oppression; there are few men who would not suffer tyranny much more readily from their own than from the stranger. When the Sultan of that day, 340 years ago, entered Syria, he found the country equally divided between Christians and Mahometans, so that if the population were three millions, as it was, one million and a half were Christians, and one million and a half Mahometans. Perhaps some of you may ask what kind of Christians they were, to what sect, to what creed did they belong. They were divided into two bodies, of which the miserable wrecks exist. The first was the Maronite population, who, as you know, having from their attachment to the Catholic Church, remained faithful, from the earliest ages of the Church, to the faith of Peter and the See of Peter, were made the subject of such bitter persecutions as had obliged them to fly from Mesopotamia and seek refuge in the rocks of Mount Lebanon, where they established themselves, defying from their rugged heights, and narrow passes the rage of the enemy. They cut down the cedar woods, which rendered the Lebanon a waste, they cultivated the rocks, and formed a well-organized and happy nation in the midst of those mountains, which were formerly mere desolation. And these mountains they held, I mean the whole of northern and central Lebanon; they remained gathered into this spot, having created a civil and religious governor of its nation, and contrary to what some people say about uniting both qualities in one man, the Maronites while under his rule remained very happy and prosperous, grew and multiplied for the space of 1200 years.

You can easily imagine that such a population as they had in the beginning, being, from the force of circumstances obliged to take up warlike habits, to take up habits of self defence, to protect their lives and properties, and being obliged to undergo frequent conflicts to keep their kingdom, you can easily understand how they deserved that character for courage and vigour by which they were known. They were a sword-bearing population these Maronites of Mount Lebanon, and while they wielded the sword of the true faith, they wielded also the literal and martial sword, by which they sustained it. They were the strength, the centre of refuge of the Christians in Syria. In that part of Mount Lebanon was to be found not only the Maronite patriarch, but also the Armenian patriarch, the Greek patriarch, and Syrian patriarch, all of whom had sought refuge in Lebanon. They were the principal in importance from their number in the division of its population. They were the principal also from another reason. They had never swerved from the true faith, and never consequently diminished their own energy, for the energy of man is knit by his persevering adherence to the faith of his forefathers. The larger number was composed of Syrians and Greeks. These Syrians belonged to that class of Christians who, while holding the Catholic faith from the beginning, at the same time have their prayers and mass, and everything else in the Syrian language, in the same way as we have ours in the Latin language. Their churches, and their altars, and their prayers, and their mass resembled ours. A great number of these Syrians had fallen into heresy, the heresy of Eutyches who, while maintaining the divinity of the Lord, denied the reality of His

Incarnation. Of these heretics, for such they were, a very large number have in later times, in my own time, and in some instances under my hands, returned to the centre of the Catholic faith, repudiated the dreadful error into which they had been led through ignorance, blindness, or bad feeling, and returned to the true faith, and were called Syrian Catholics. They formed a large mass of its population. Many villages, containing upwards of four or five thousand inhabitants, situated on the edge of the Syrian desert, were composed of them. As for the Greeks you are well acquainted with them. I am not speaking to an uneducated but an educated audience, and there is no need to say how they have fallen into schism from the Church. However, in our day also, a very large body of them returned to the true faith, to the centre of holy unity; and at the time when I myself, though unworthy, was fulfilling the duties of Catholic missionary, I was able to count 60,000. So far this population of Greeks and Syrians were not formidable to the Mahometans and Turks from military strength. They were what are called townspeople, which had a different meaning in the east from what it bears here, for the luxury, the high living, the easy life, enervate the martial spirit of the population, so that no soldier could be enlisted from the townsmen of the east, no matter whether he is Mahometan or Christian, and the whole strength of the country consequently lies in the peasantry and mountaineers. You know already that all this country which I have been describing, up to the moment of the Turkish invasion, was divided between Mahometans and Christians of different orders, being so divided into three belts, the first of which was occupied by the Bedouins and Maronites, the second by the Syrians, and the third by the remainder of the population.

It would be needless for me to go through a description of the neighbours of these Maronites, and how they are derived from the Druses, of which every one knows the term, and very few the reality. Of the thousands of Christians who inhabit Syria, I hardly met one who really knew their belief or practice. However, we have in our time, and very lately, discovered their belief; and I myself, owing to peculiar circumstances, have been enabled not only to confirm what they have stated, but to add to it, and the result of my investigation, living among them as one who found himself, not in a polemical position, but as an intimate friend, as one coming from the land of India, whence I came, and I was able to discover many points in them I never saw stated; the result is, that I believe the nation of Druses are simply a nation of atheists—nothing less. Though, by a singular inconsistency, they admit the existence of spirits, they still deny the immortality of any spirits, whether the spirits of men or disembodied spirits; and they also deny the existence of a supreme uncreated Being. These people, formerly

inhabited Egypt, and, after falling into this gulf through circumstances too long to relate, but which would be highly interesting
and instructive, if any one had time to lecture upon them, they
settled in Mount Lebanon, at least eight hundred years since, and
became the neighbours of the Maronites, with whom they lived on
very good terms; for such men, having no principle of enthusiasm,
and having no object in quarreling with those of a different belief, as
they themselves believe in nothing at all, live quietly with all. However, the clashing of different interests and the events which always
happen between next-door neighbours would, from time to time,
bring on some slight and unimportant war. As to these tribes of
the Christians, they are very little known to you; but all of them
are distinct from the great body of the Mahometan race. At the
first entrance of the Ottoman power into Syria, the number of
Christians was, at least, half the population. At the time of the
war in the Crimea, and in 1856, the number of Christians in Syria,
instead of being half, was not more than one-sixth part of the
population. How, you will ask, could such a change have been
brought about? In a word, by the systematic course of oppression,
of slaughter, of bondage, and of blood and murder, carried on by
the Ottoman Government for the space of 340 years, without pause,
without intermission. I myself have spoken to many who have
witnessed scenes of the most cruel torture, in the same way as some
of you may have heard from your grandfathers or your fathers,
certain details of oppression in your own country. I will give you
an instance. One of the most influential and respectable men in
Tripoli—he is advanced in years now—related to me how his father
was seized one day by order of the Turkish governor, taken from
his home, and cast into a dungeon, and variously tormented for
several days, for no other reason than that he had wealth hoarded
in his house which he was unwilling to hand over, without a receipt
from the Pacha. Having been compelled, by the force of torture,
to give up this money, which he had acquired by his own industry,
they suspecting that he had not given all, caused a fire to be lighted
in the midst of the prison, placed a large cauldron in the centre of
it, and flung him into it. The insufferable agony obliged him to
disclose where his last farthing was concealed, and then they permitted him to be carried back to his own home, where he died that
very evening. It was this man's own son who related to me this
fact. But this is only a solitary, casual fact. Hundreds, thousands
of other acts, equal to it, have taken place. There was a man
who held acres at the time Napoleon the First entered Syria, who
having been on the point of being driven out by the French emperor,
was upheld in the country by the influence of a government which
should never have supported such a man—however, he was sup-

ported, and he maintained his post by means of British aid—this man I heard myself, while the fortifications were being built, walked daily around them, and any one, especially a Christian, who displeased him in look or in manner, he would order to be built alive into the wall, so that he actually raised the fortifications of the place in human blood. Such was the Turkish Government for an uninterrupted series of 340 years. Is it strange if the Christian population diminished under such an abominable system of tyranny? Numbers and numbers, who could do so, emigrated, and happy were those who had the means. Some of them, certainly, apostatised from the faith to escape from torture and death; but thousands and thousands perished by the sword, preferring death to apostasy, and gained the crown of martyrdom. There were over 1,750 in Lebanon who fell victims to the Turkish daggers, whether used by the hands of the Turks or by those of the Druses. From the date of the war in Sebastopol, and the peace which followed it, and the treaty which was solemnly made, ratified, signed, and published in Europe and America, it became impossible for the Turkish Government to carry on the process of extermination at which she was employed, and she was obliged to give a sort of outside varnish which should hide her horrible cruelty. This varnish, this veil was too transparent to conceal the real feelings of the inhabitants, and from the very outset a voice was raised that since it was impossible to treat Christians as Christian dogs should be treated, it was necessary to bring matters to a short and speedy end. However, the pressure of persecution being off, the true faith multiplied. But this state of things did not last long. Allow me to place before you one spot in the country—the city of Damascus—in which I lived myself for a short time, and in connexion with which I have lately appeared before the public. In that city, which is, without contradiction, the loveliest city on the face of the globe, situated beneath the mountains, from which the famous rivers of Damascus pour down the rugged side through it until not a home is without its water font, not a street in which there are not to be seen fountains, with the water playing and sparkling in them before the eyes of the inhabitants—a city embosomed in gardens which men on horseback could not pass through in less than three or four hours, so extensive are they—a city so adorned with all that Asiatic luxury and splendour could supply, that the new city of Damascus has passed into a proverb—where are to be seen houses built of marble and precious stones, whose balls, nearly as large as this in which we stand, would not be raised one inch above the ground, without having rare marble and precious stones inserted in them—a city where civilization and luxury have been carried to the highest pitch—a city in which have been raised lately, in our own time, almost under my own eyes (for they were only built four or five years before I entered it, and the walls were quite fresh when I arrived there) a magnificent church by the Greek Catholic population of Damascus, in which the faithful assembled daily, but more especially at the customary periods, to the number of 6,000, to offer up prayers to God; close to it, of equally recent date, a Syrian Church, containing 2,000; close to that a Church of the Maronites, in which were no small number of the faithful; besides a convent of the Sisters of Mercy; a convent of the Fathers of St. Vincent de Paul, and a convent of the Basilian Monks, so that whoever entered it would say this is a Christian town, and not only a Christian but a Catholic town, and not only a Catholic but a flourishing Catholic town. I myself, as I had occasion to say once before, on the 30th of April last, a few months since, and just twenty-seven days before the outbreak, was called on by my bishop to preach the first sermon on the opening of a new Catholic Church erected by the bishops in a part of the town which was never used by Christians. Over 1,200 Christians were assembled in that quarter of the city, and I myself, on the 30th of April, preached the opening sermon in the new church there, when the bishop consecrated it and said the first Mass. You all know how the destruction of the city of Damascus was brought about. Imagine that you stand on Mount Lebanon, overlooking the plain of Damascus, and that you see the town with its 150,000 inhabitants —imagine the Christian quarter to be the most brilliant, the most highly ornamented, the most thickly populated of the whole place, adorned with its churches, its monuments, its institutions, containing at the outbreak 24,000 people, 4,000 having sought it for refuge— imagine you see it shining in the morning sun, its fountains sparkling, its palaces, its gardens—imagine that you see all these, and then imagine that you see it at the present moment (I see it still) that whole quarter one blank—not a broken wall, not a ruined house, not a desecrated church remaining, but a mere blank, for at the present moment there is not a wall at the height even of this table from the ground—the whole is levelled to the dust. Such has been the conduct of the Turkish Government to the most faithful subjects on earth, who never disputed an order from Constantinople, who professed, with all respect to the Government, their own religion, and worshipped God according to the faith of their forefathers, who never gave the slightest provocation to the Mahometans, who, from the very outset, had shown great disposition to submit to any thing, who even refrained from taking up arms in self-defence lest it might be said they gave occasion to provoke this war. After all there have been found men to stand before the assembled nations, and say the origin and cause of the war was the fault of the Christians. Incredible falsehood, which the facts will deny, not alone at the present day, but to the end of time. Were you in the country you would see the streams empurpled with the gore of the inhabitants, many of them slain for their money. You would hear the wail of 10,000 exiles rushing to the sea-coast, seeking the protection of Europe. You would hear the groan and wail of others who are unable to drag themselves along, and who die on the road by hundreds and thousands. You should see the tears, you should hear the wail. Who can express the feelings of the 200 women and maidens in the arms of the very men who murdered their fathers, their husbands, their brothers, for no less than 200 are prisoners at the present moment. You should see the corpses mingled with the ashes of the habitations. Such is the result of Turkish government, of Turkish protection, of Turkish civilization. Very many nations have not ceased to insult us for the last four years with the word, "Turkish civilization." If you desire to see Turkish civilization, look at the city of Damascus. Should you wish to know how this state of things was brought about, I will give you, in a few words, some of the principal events, which have been misunderstood by those who receive their information from the press of a neighbouring country. The facts were these, and I can bear witness to them, having myself been present at Damascus, at the beginning of the outbreak, and having heard the rest from eye witnesses, and not only that, I received letters (I being in the mountains) from my friends in Damascus, who gave me accounts day by day of what was going on around them, until the 8th July, when all communication ceased, and I do not know where the writers are—whether in this or the next world. However, the events passed in this manner: After the war had broken out in Lebanon, and the public voice declared in Damascus—and I myself heard it—that after the Turkish fanatics should have succeeded in annihilating, by means of the Druses, whatever remnant of Christianity and Catholicity remained in the East, by hurling a mass of barbarous assassins, without shame or fear of God, on the unprepared population of Lebanon; after they have done there, the next blow will be to occupy the entire of the country, and first Damascus. You can imagine with what consternation the inhabitants received the news of that fatal order. On the 27th of May, a night which, if I had not witnessed, I would not believe ever occurred, forty defenceless villages, containing between three and four thousand Catholics, were reduced to ashes, the inhabitants driven away or massacred, whilst the Turkish governor sat quietly in the midst of the smoking villages, contemplating the massacres, directing and encouraging the murderers. Two days after four masses of Druses were let in at different points, to Damascus, while the inhabitants were wholly unprepared, and let those hear it who say the Christians were the cause of the war; they not only razed the town to the earth, but slaughtered fully a thousand of the population, drove another thousand into a neighbouring wood, and with a cruelty that may have found a parallel in some parts of Ireland in old times, set fire to the wood, where the thousand had taken refuge, and not one of them escaped from the flames. Of those who remained, and they were fully two thousand, the men were butchered, the women insulted, the priests tortured, and the monks and nuns put to the same punishment. From the beginning of the war the Christians of Damascus knew the feelings of the Mahometan inhabitants were against them. I knew one, I lodged in his house, and he was one of the worthiest of men, who went down on his knees to a Mahometan, to beg him to allow his wife and children to take refuge in his dwelling, in case the massacre should take place on that night. The men would not beg their own lives. The inhabitants of the largest Christian village in the southern part of Mount Lebanon, renowned for their courage and generous spirit, the inhabitants of this village—if one can call it a village—which contains 6,000 inhabitants, and large schools for boys and girls, and if you ask me where the masters are, I can tell you that the bones of two of them whiten the ashes of the school, and that the third escaped; they, after having repelled the attack of the Druses, who were three times more numerous than themselves, and provided by the government with ammunition, while the Christians were kept without arms, without powder, without food, so that many of them remained for three days suffering the horrors of hunger, after they had repelled the attack for this period, they at last gave themselves up, the Turkish governor promising on the most solemn oath that he would defend them, and would not suffer a hair of their heads to be injured. But, with a fiendish treachery, which was only equalled in Wexford, when the inhabitants, to the number of 3,000, had been received into the spacious palace of the governor, where he brought them ostensibly for their greater protection, but in reality that he might have the pleasure of seeing them butchered, then and there the doors were thrown open, and the Christians led out one by one, while the Druses, with hatchets and axes and swords, and the implements of vilest butchery, massacred them almost to the very last. Only fifteen escaped. One of these I saw the moment he arrived at Beyrout, and I could not recognise him, so changed was he by the horrors he had undergone. When these massacres took place under the eye of the Turkish governor, what could the inhabitants of Damascus expect but the same or worse treatment? Their expectations were not wrong. A few days after, the governor of Damascus, who holds the same position in Syria as the highest magistrate does in Ireland, who holds his nomination and receives his orders from the Sultan himself, this man—if man one could call him—as if he took a fiendish pleasure in making his victims taste all the agonies of fear, called the Druses, the very men who killed their Christian brethren, to "defend" the quarters of the Christians. They occupied the houses, sat at the tables of the Christians, and from such a beginning it was not hard to see how matters would go on. All arms were taken from the Christians, the Druses, on the contrary, were supplied with every description of weapon, and the cannon of the fort were pointed to the houses of the Christian quarter. The firing of these was the signal for the soldiery to descend from the fort, and occupy the only outlets for the Christians—the eastern gate and the gate of St. Thomas. Every ruffian, every bandit, every Druse, with hatchet reeking with blood, who presented himself, was allowed to pass; but every Christian who attempted to escape from the spreading flames, or the blood-stained hatchet, were driven back on their assassins and the fire, until the ancient river, mentioned in Holy Writ, was literally choked with corpses. You might have heard how the governor was seated on the roof of his palace, a new Nero, smoking his pipe, enjoying the spectacle, and calling on the band to play the liveliest airs. I will record only one circumstance which has been "burked" by the press of a certain country. I have the information on the very best authority, that of an official, a former friend of mine, who had been deputed by the five European consuls at Beyrout, to give notice of what was happening in Damascus. He said to me: "About one hour from the gate of Damascus, passing by a village which contains 2000 inhabitants, more or less, of which the Christians number only two or three hundred, I was surprised to see it utterly silent. I had passed it three days before, and there was no change in the appearance of the place. Well, when I came to the market-place, where there is a large trunk of tree lying on the ground, and used as a seat by the villagers, I saw it in a pool of blood, and around it were the bodies of two hundred Christians, men and women, who had all been decapitated, one by one, on the trunk." The Turkish assassins, after this horrid deed, had gone to take share in the massacres at Damascus. There is not a part of the land, for the extent of at least half of Ireland, that has not been desolated. Draw a line from Dublin to Galway, and imagine at the present moment there is not a single convent, a single person to make the sign of the cross in that whole country, and you have an idea of the state of central Syria at this moment.

I cannot any longer dwell on these matters, and I am happy that this is the last evening that I shall have occasion to speak of them publicly, because, after those scenes occurred I was for a long time unable to speak about them, and even at the present moment,

when I picture them it is too much for me. What I have said will
suffice; and I consider that you are in duty and honour bound to
your fellow Christians and Catholics, to give those facts all the
publicity in your power. I will only say, before parting, that you
should consider what have been the consequences of this outbreak.
You can picture to yourself the country, inhabited at one time
principally by Catholics, but in which Turkish treachery and cruelty
have now reduced them to a minority. I leave it to yourselves to
conceive the number of orphans, of widows, of houseless, roofless, and
dying men, women, and children, that are at present wandering over
the deserts of Syria, or would vainly seek to return to the ashes of
their once happy homes. I would only represent one circumstance to
which I have already alluded, but it cannot be too often spoken of.
Our Blessed Lord and Redeemer said once to His disciples, and to all
Catholics: " Fear not him who can kill the body, and after that can
do no more; but fear Him who, after having slain the body, can cast
the body and soul into hell-fire." The death of this body is of very
slight consequence; but there is another death, more fearful than
the death of the body, it is the death of the soul. It is the extinc-.
tion of faith, it is apostasy from his religion and mother Church,
it is that entry into the way of endless death. That is the danger to
which the remnants of the Christian population in Syria are exposed by a system of proselytizing invented by the demon himself,
carried out with fiendish perseverance, partly by the Mahometans
and partly by others—a system of relief which would pretend to be
charitable, but which is only given on condition that the person
receiving it passes from the holy Catholic faith to the creed of
Mahomet and other forms of delusion and false doctrine. That system is being carried on to a great extent in Syria, and unless it be
met, and promptly met, it will have deadly results, seeing that the
misery of the people will be increased during the coming winter.

These are facts that I have laid before you. Whatever conclusion may be drawn from them I leave to yourselves. I confide in the sympathy of your Catholic breasts and the generosity
of your Irish hearts, that what has been said will not be without its fruits and blessing, not only to the inhabitants of Syria,
by exerting your charity to assist them, but will also bring upon
the inhabitants of Cork, and of all Ireland, the rewards promised
by God for acts of charity done to our neighbour.

EXTRACT FROM A LETTER RECEIVED BY THE REV. FATHER PALGRAVE, WRITTEN BY ONE OF HIS CONFRERES AT BEYROUT.

"Beyrout, 31st, August.

" The Druses continue to kill the Christians wherever they meet them, and they cut down the mulberry trees and carry off all the wood work of the Christian's houses. They have sold all the vintage of the Christians of Syria. Since the date of the arrival of Fuad Pasha, 16th July, they have persecuted the Christians whereever they met them, have killed eleven of them, and carried off a large amount of property. The names of the victims and of their villages are now before me. Since the same date, twelve Christians have been killed in the direction of Baalbeck by the Metualis. We cannot understand why Fuad Pasha has let them go on in this way, and allowed the Christian villages and their lands to remain a prey to the Druses, without giving these poor people sufficient protection to enable them to return to their own dwellings. The people of Gezzim did return to their own district, but were in a few days driven away to Beyrout again. The French soldiers found close to their camp at the pine wood, a small church entirely filled with dead bodies of Christians, amongst which were several bodies of Maronite clergy, and children, quartered. These dead bodies were quite fresh, and were evidently massacred since the wars.

" You must not allow yourself to think that Fuad Pasha did much at Damascus. He did put 160 to death, but of the whole lot there were only three or four men of any note amongst the Mussulmans of Damascus, the others were all unfortunate poor who were got together, and were previously half dead of hunger. The Mussulmans would not restore to the Christians the property they had plundered. All the furniture and wood work was employed in heating the baths, and the rest was thrown into the two rivers.

" Full information of this destruction was given to Fuad Pasha every morning for six days, yet he did not interfere. Some mats, blankets, bedding, and copper pots were returned to Fuad Pasha for distribution amongst the Christians. The bad and worthless were returned, the others were kept. All that was old and dirty in the furniture of the Mussulman houses was given them. Scarce anything that was of the least value was restored. A few days ago, 300 of the murderers of Damascus arrived bound, at Beyrout, and were embarked for Constantinople. As they were being marched into Beyrout, a Turk said to the Christians, "Don't rejoice at that, they are merely going to Constantinople to put on the soldier's dress, and then they will return to complete the work they have commenced." On arriving on board ship their chains were removed. Several others were seized by Fuad Pasha and made soldiers ; and it is quite a lucky chance for this unfortunate empire to find an opportunity of seizing many people for soldiers. Just think of what is being done at Damascus, and through the rest of the Ottoman empire. In all the towns there are troops of assassins and murderers. You remember, I think, the military Caimacam at Beteddin. In 1850 he was the head of the assassins who attacked the Christians of Aleppo, and for this deed he was promoted in the army of the Sultan. After Kars he was further promoted and made Caimacam of Beteddin ; he was the head of the band who massacred 2114 Christians at that place, and at Deir el Kamer. What can be expected from such troops? Two regiments of soldiers of the Turkish army, the other day, began to beat the Christians of Damascus, now seeking refuge at Beyrout, as they were going out to bathe. Some Zouaves saw them and took them prisoners, and handed them over to the government.

"There is much to apprehend for Palestine and for Aleppo also Yesterday we read news from Acre that the Turks had made crosses on the doors of the churches with human excrement, and also made small crosses, which they put on the ground, and forcing the Christians to stand by and witness their outrage, they made water upon the crosses. Six thousand French will never be sufficient to do much, and the Turkish troops only hinder their being able to act. We should need 40,000 at least. If the French do not act energetically at once, independent of the Turks, we shall have great misery for a long time; and if ever the French leave the country, we shall have more terrible massacres than ever. We are now more execrated and hated by all the infidels than ever before. No one dares now to think of rebuilding their ruined houses."

www.ingramcontent.com/pod-product-compliance
Lightning Source LLC
Chambersburg PA
CBHW021548270326
41930CB00008B/1410